"Kevin DeYoung writes with inspiring clarity [...] mons a generation of Christians to courage an[...] choice that matters most is actually a lifetime [...] book to give to your graduating high school and college students. But please don't pigeonhole this book. *Do Not Be True to Yourself* is a brilliant and succinct call to all Christians to reject the spirit of the age in favor of the courageous Christian faith."

Rosaria Butterfield, Former Professor of English, Syracuse University; author, *The Gospel Comes with a House Key*

"Kevin DeYoung's *Do Not Be True to Yourself* is a helpful antidote to a culture of self-obsession. If we're learning anything about human nature in the age in which we live, it is that outsized focus on oneself produces disabling anxiety, disorienting 'identities,' and dizzying confusion about man's ultimate end. It turns out, secular man's chief end of glorifying himself is producing the very opposite of joy. This book shows why and shows a better, godward way forward."

Andrew T. Walker, Associate Professor of Christian Ethics, The Southern Baptist Theological Seminary

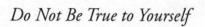

Do Not Be True to Yourself

Do Not Be True to Yourself

Countercultural Advice for the Rest of Your Life

Kevin DeYoung

WHEATON, ILLINOIS

Published in association with the literary agency of Wolgemuth & Associates, Inc.

Cover design: Jordan Singer

First printing 2023

Printed in the United States of America

Unless otherwise indicated, Scripture quotations are from the ESV® Bible (The Holy Bible, English Standard Version®), copyright © 2001 by Crossway, a publishing ministry of Good News Publishers. Used by permission. All rights reserved. The ESV text may not be quoted in any publication made available to the public by a Creative Commons license. The ESV may not be translated into any other language.

Scripture quotations marked NIV are taken from the Holy Bible, New International Version®, NIV®. Copyright © 1973, 1978, 1984, 2011 by Biblica, Inc.™ Used by permission of Zondervan. All rights reserved worldwide. www.zondervan.com. The "NIV" and "New International Version" are trademarks registered in the United States Patent and Trademark Office by Biblica, Inc.™

Scripture quotations marked NLT are taken from the Holy Bible, New Living Translation, copyright © 1996, 2004, 2015 by Tyndale House Foundation. Used by permission of Tyndale House Publishers, a Division of Tyndale House Ministries, Carol Stream, Illinois 60188. All rights reserved.

All emphases in Scripture quotations have been added by the author.

Trade paperback ISBN: 978-1-4335-9005-4
ePub ISBN: 978-1-4335-9008-5
PDF ISBN: 978-1-4335-9006-1
Mobipocket ISBN: 978-1-4335-9007-8

Library of Congress Cataloging-in-Publication Data

Names: DeYoung, Kevin, author.
Title: Do not be true to yourself : countercultural advice for the rest of
   your life / Kevin DeYoung.
Description: Wheaton, Illinois : Crossway, 2023. | Includes bibliographical
   references and index.
Identifiers: LCCN 2022041416 (print) | LCCN 2022041417 (ebook) | ISBN 9781433590054
   (trade paperback) | ISBN 9781433590061 (pdf) | ISBN 9781433590085 (epub)
Subjects: LCSH: Christian life. | Virtues. | Philosophy of mind. | Theology, Practical.
Classification: LCC BV4501.3 .D496 2023 (print) | LCC BV4501.3 (ebook) | DDC 248.4--dc23/
   eng/20230112
LC record available at https://lccn.loc.gov/2022041416
LC ebook record available at https://lccn.loc.gov/2022041417

To Ian,
our firstborn and the first to leave for college,
we love you and miss you.

Contents

Introduction

IN MAY 2022, I had the privilege of giving the commencement address at Geneva College (Beaver Falls, PA). I didn't want to recycle the usual commencement fare: "Follow your dreams! Be all that you can be! Go out and change the world!" Instead, I decided to give the opposite sort of advice, as you'll see when you read the first chapter of this book. A few weeks later, I gave the same basic message at the baccalaureate service for Covenant Day School (the school associated with my church). I then posted the Geneva commencement address online.

To my pleasant surprise, the message seemed to resonate with a lot of people. Besides getting a good following online, I heard from pastors and friends and Christians in various places who appreciated the countercultural sentiment. About a month later, Justin Taylor from Crossway asked if I would consider publishing that talk in a little booklet. The plan for a little booklet then morphed into this little book.

Over the years I've preached at a number of baccalaureate services and commencement services. I've also preached targeted sermons to high school or college students just beginning or just ending their studies. I've collected some of those messages here, retaining much of the spoken style so you can "hear" the message as well as read it. If there is a theme that holds the chapters together it is the simple exhortation to serve God faithfully and counterculturally in the next season of your life. Obviously, if you have just finished high school or college or some other milestone as a young adult, these messages will speak to your situation. This book is especially for you. But insofar as the counsel in these pages is biblical, I think Christians (and maybe even non-Christians) of all ages can read the book with profit.

May God help us to live by his Spirit, according to his word, and for his glory—as young people, as middle-agers like me, and every stage of Christian discipleship.

1

Don't Be True to Yourself

TWENTY YEARS AGO, Anna Quindlen—a writer for the *New York Times*, a Pulitzer Prize winner, and a recipient of prestigious honorary degrees—gave this advice to a group of graduating seniors:

Each of you is as different as your fingertips. Why should you march to any lockstep? Our love of lockstep is our greatest curse, the source of all that bedevils us. It is the source of homophobia, xenophobia, racism, sexism, terrorism, bigotry of every variety and hue because it tells us that there is one right way to do things, to look, to behave, to feel, when the only right way is to feel your heart hammering inside you and to listen to what its timpani is saying.[1]

That's fairly typical commencement counsel: "Follow your dreams. March to the beat of your own drummer. Be true to yourself."[2]

I'd like to offer different advice: "Do not follow your dreams. Do not march to the beat of your own drummer. And whatever you do, do *not* be true to yourself."

If you think I'm being a little hyperbolic, you're right. I'll provide some nuance to this advice at the end. But I believe it's important to state the matter provocatively because our world screams at us in thousands of commercials, movies, and songs that the best way to live, the *only authentic* way to live, is for you to be you, for you to live out *your* truth, for you to find your true self and then have the courage to live accordingly.

Deceived by Desires

The Bible, on the other hand, tells us, "There is a way that seems right to a man, but its end is the way of death" (Prov. 14:12). Think of the story of Esau who sold his birthright for a pot of stew. "Let me eat some of that red stew," he said, "for I am exhausted. I am about to die; of what use is a birthright to me?" (Gen. 25:30, 32). Esau was consumed with his desires.

Esau was defined by his desires, and they deceived him. Esau is depicted as an animal. You can see this more clearly in the original Hebrew. All he can think of is the red stuff, the red stuff (*ha-adom, ha-adom*). He exaggerates the extent of his need. He wasn't literally going to die. (Like kids saying when dinner is a half hour late, "I'm starving!"). Esau is emotional and impulsive. He is fainting, gasping, gulping. You can almost see him wiping off his mouth, throwing down a napkin, and letting out a loud belch as he walks away from his meal of stew. He was not made nobler for satisfying his desires. He was made lower. He became like an animal. That's what the text wants us to see. Esau the skillful hunter was prey to his own appetites. He had a better identity as the firstborn of Isaac, but he gave that away. He became a profane man, treating what was sacred with irreverence and disrespect.

The world tells us that our identity is found in what we desire. So to deny the fulfillment of what you desire is to deny your truest identity. We are all awash in what Carl Trueman calls "expressive individualism."[3] The idea is that you are what you feel, and don't let anyone tell you otherwise. I'm sure you remember Elsa's anthem "Let It Go" from *Frozen*. With its emphasis on testing the limits and breaking through, it's no wonder the song and the character Elsa have become a favorite in the LGBTQ+ community.

No right, no wrong, no rules for me
I'm free.[4]

What could be more indicative of the spirit of the age?

A Philosophy for Our Times

Throughout most of history, philosophers and theologians have distinguished between affections (which are motions of the will) and passions (which sweep over us unbidden). That's why the Westminster Confession says God is without parts and passions. The Westminster divines were using "passion" not as we do to mean intense zeal. They were saying, God does not have an emotional life like we do. He is Pure Act; nothing happens *to* him. He is never rendered passive.

Consequently, the Western tradition, especially in the Christian tradition, has insisted that the lower appetites must be constrained by reason and the grace of God working within us. In fact, the Reformed tradition goes one step further and reminds us that we can be misled by all our faculties. That's what we mean by the phrase "totally depraved"—our passions are broken, our reason is not entirely reliable, and our wills, apart from Christ, are bound to sin.

Most people you will encounter in life—and maybe you, reading this today—operate with an unspoken assumption that shapes and defines every argument, every instinct, and the way you look at the world and look at yourself. The assumption is this: *is equals ought*. Importantly, the *is* here is no longer about your body. It's not about some physical givenness. "My body tells me something true about myself even when I don't feel that it is true." That mindset is no longer assumed. Now it is assumed that what you feel about yourself, or believe about yourself, or perceive about yourself tells you who you are and how you should behave.

Is equals ought conditions us to believe: "This is what I feel like, so this is what I should do; and if you tell me I can't do that, or that I should be something or someone other than I feel myself to be, you are attacking the very heart of my personhood."

What's wrong with this philosophical assumption? Besides being devoid of any objective, empirical, scientific facts, the assumption is entirely at odds with Christian anthropology. The only way *is equals ought* can work is if there is no doctrine of the fall—if our instincts are never self-deceived, if our desires are never self-centered, and if our dreams are never self-destructive.

The salvation we all know we need is not to be found by looking within ourselves but by looking for grace outside ourselves. G. K. Chesterton said it so well:

That Jones shall worship the god within him turns out ultimately to mean that Jones shall worship Jones. Let Jones worship the sun or moon, anything rather than the Inner Light; let Jones worship cats or crocodiles, if he can find any in his street, but not the god within. Christianity came into the world firstly in order to assert with violence that a man had not only to look inwards, but to look outwards, to behold with astonishment and enthusiasm a divine company and a divine captain. The only fun of being a Christian was that a man was not left alone with the Inner Light, but definitely recognized an outer light, fair as the sun, clear as the moon, terrible as an army with banners.[5]

Like most heresies, the *is equals ought* heresy is partially true. It grasps something we want to affirm; namely, that ethics must be rooted in ontology. That's just a fancy way of saying identity does shape obligation. Is *does* equal ought, *if* you have a doctrine of sin, regeneration, union with Christ, and the indwelling of the Holy Spirit. The great theologian of our age, Lady Gaga, was right: you were born that way. The good news of Jesus Christ is that you can be born again another way.

A Tale of Two Films

Think about two Pixar movies that came out ten years apart. In a movie review for *World* magazine, Collin Garbarino recently pointed out the difference between the movie *Brave* (2012) and the movie *Turning Red* (2022).[6] Both movies are coming-of-age mother-daughter stories. In both movies, the daughters feel constrained by their overbearing mothers. In both movies, the mom gets turned into an angry, out-of-control animal.

In *Turning Red*, the message is more about self-actualization, how we all have a messy side we need to let out. The daughter tells her mom, "My panda, my body"[7] (echoing the slogan "my body, my choice"), and we are supposed to accept that the daughter (who can turn into a red panda) is right to chart her own path as long as she is true to herself.

But if you remember, the narrative arc in *Brave* was much different. There, the mother and the daughter realize they have both been proud. The torn tapestry is a symbol of their broken relationship, and they must "mend the bond torn by pride."[8] The lesson in *Brave* is about learning to say "sorry." It's a fun adventure movie that is really about repentance, forgiveness, and change. It's about how being true to yourself can get you in trouble and hurt those around you.

Recall that line from Anna Quindlen: "The only right way [to behave] is to feel your heart hammering inside you and to listen to what its timpani is saying."[9] Rich Mullins offered a better way in his song, "The Maker of Noses." After describing the dead end of following your heart and following your dreams, Mullins testifies that: "The Father of hearts and the

Maker of noses / and the giver of dreams [is] the one I have chosen / and I will follow Him."[10]

Be Who You Are, but Die First

There is something right about our culture's obsession with authenticity. One of the chief ethical motivations in the New Testament is: be who you are. Which is why my provocative statement ("do not be true to yourself") at the beginning needs some qualification. You should not be true to yourself, unless you have died to your old self and your new self is raised with Christ and seated with him in the heavenly places. The real you *is* worth letting out *if* the real you is dead to sin and alive in Christ Jesus.

The world says you are what you feel. The world says your *is equals ought*. The world says you must find yourself, be true to yourself, and express yourself. Jesus gave us a different and better way to live.

> Truly, truly, I say to you, unless a grain of wheat falls into the earth and dies, it remains alone; but if it dies, it bears much fruit. Whoever loves his life loses it, and whoever hates his life in this world will keep it for eternal life. (John 12:24–25)

2

Choose for Yourselves

THE BOOK OF JOSHUA is about conquest, how God not only delivered his people from Egypt, but also led them into the promised land. If you remember the book, you remember all the battles, at Jericho and Ai, and all the kings they defeated, and then chapter after chapter of land allotments to the twelve tribes. The book is about the conquest of Canaan, which is why the beginning of Joshua 23 is so striking: "After a long time had passed and the Lord had given Israel rest from all their enemies . . ." (23:1 NIV). Israel was finally at rest.

The Israelites had control and possession of (much of) Canaan. The battles had been fought, and their enemies had been subdued. Joshua was going to pass from the scene, so in Joshua 23, he gathered the leaders for his farewell. Then in Joshua 24, Joshua gathered all the tribes and their leaders at Shechem to renew the covenant. This is the covenant between God and Israel originally ratified in Exodus 24, the covenant arrangement was that God would be their God and they would worship him and obey his commands. Long before Billy Graham's crusades, they were having a recommitment service.

In Joshua 24, Joshua begins by reminding Israel of their history. More accurately, he reminds them of God's history, but their history is the story of God's work among them. Joshua speaks for God, as if to say:

- *Remember* the patriarchs. Your ancestors were idolaters, but I gave them a new home and gave them descendants like the stars in the sky. I did that for you.
- *Remember* Moses and Aaron. You were slaves in Egypt. I sent the plagues. I parted the Red Sea. I swallowed up the Egyptians.
- *Remember* before you entered the promised land, I destroyed the Amorites, I frustrated the plans of Balak.
- *Remember* when you entered Canaan, I parted the Jordan for you and destroyed your enemies. I gave you a land in which you did not build and did not plant. I did all this for you.

The people of Israel probably enjoyed this rehearsal of their history. "Amen, Joshua. That's right! The Lord has been our God, and ours alone! Go on!" But Joshua doesn't leave them there to simply celebrate their history, he challenges them: "Now therefore fear the Lord and serve him in sincerity and faithfulness. Put away the gods that your fathers served beyond the River and in Egypt, and serve the Lord" (24:14). It's not enough to revel in your history, Joshua says. What about now? If the Lord your God did all this for you, then serve Him *alone*.

Choose This Day

After the challenge, Joshua gives the people a choice, where he effectively says, "If one of these other gods is true, then by all means, serve that god. And if it is evil in your eyes to serve the Lord, then don't do it. But you can't ride the fence on this one." Then Joshua utters those famous words, which have made their way onto many plaques in many homes (including mine): "But as for me and my house, we will serve the Lord" (24:15).

Don't you admire Joshua? I want to be a Joshua. I want to stand up and be counted, to live for something and maybe even die for something. I pray for this kind of courage when my convictions are on the line. I want to be like Martin

Luther before the Diet of Worms: "I cannot and will not recant." Or like Eric Liddell before the 1924 Olympics: "I will not run." Or like Peter and John before the Sanhedrin:

> Let it be known to all of you and to all the people of Israel that by the name of Jesus Christ of Nazareth, whom you crucified, whom God raised from the dead—by him this man is standing before you well. . . . And there is salvation in no one else, for there is no other name under heaven given among men by which we must be saved. (Acts 4:10, 12)

Choose for yourselves whom you will serve, but as for me and my house, we will serve the Lord.

The Israelites seemed to give a great answer to Joshua's challenge: "Far be it from us that we should forsake the Lord to serve other gods" (Josh. 24:16). They recognized that it was the Lord who brought them out of Egypt. It was the Lord who drove out the Amorites. "Therefore," they concluded, "we also will serve the Lord, for he is our God" (v. 18).

Then Joshua responded by saying, "Praise the Lord. That is so wonderful. I'm glad you gave your life to Yahweh. I hope to see you in church next Sunday." Actually, that's *not at all* what Joshua said. "You are not able to serve the Lord," was

Joshua's reply, "for he is a holy God. He is a jealous God; he will not forgive your transgressions or your sins" (v. 19).

The Israelites knew the right answer. They pretty much summarized what Joshua had recounted, they agreed with the history, and without hesitation answered the challenge, "We will serve the Lord." *Come on, Joshua. We are Israelites, right? Of course, we aren't going to serve the gods of the Egyptians or Amorites. We follow the Lord!*

So why does Joshua rebuke them? Because he knew they weren't single-minded in their devotion. "Don't give me that trite answer," Joshua was saying. "I'm not going to accept a half-hearted, double-minded obedience, because God won't accept it either." Do you hear what you are saying? God will not look lightly on your rebellion."

Then the people redoubled their commitment. "No, but we will serve the Lord" (v. 21). Joshua finally relented. He basically said, "Okay, then, you have said it yourselves, that you are not going to have a foot in both camps. You are going to serve the Lord and the Lord alone. Let's see how that turns out for you."

Serious and Single-Minded

Like you and me, the Israelites knew all the right answers. It's like that joke about the Sunday school classroom. The teacher asks, "What's big, gray, has a large trunk and floppy ears."

The student answers, "It sounds like an elephant, but this is Sunday school, so I'm gonna have to say Jesus." We think we already know how to answer all the questions.

This is where this message gets tough for us, just as Joshua's words must have seemed tough on the Israelites. You see, this wasn't an evangelistic message Joshua was giving. These were people who already belonged to the community of faith. These were the kind of people who had come before the elders, made professions of faith, and belonged to a church. It is to *these* people that Joshua says, "Choose this day whom you will serve." Joshua might say to us, "You say you're a Christian. You come to church. You own a lot of Bibles. You've been to summer camp. But do you serve the Lord alone? If your friends are god, serve them. If your phone is god, serve it. If sports saved you from your sins, serve sports. If grades are going to make your life worth living, serve them. If movies and television and parties are what give your life purpose, then serve them. But if Jesus is God, then stop trying to hedge your bets."

Here's how Martyn Lloyd-Jones, one of the most famous preachers of the twentieth century, put the options:

Don't come here if you honestly feel that you could do better elsewhere. Unless you feel that something is being offered and given to you here which no other institutions can offer or equal, well then, in the name of Heaven, go out into the country or to the sea-side. The church of Christ is a church of believers and a common love. You don't believe? Well, above all, do not pretend that you do, go to the country and the sea-side. All I ask of you is, be consistent. When someone dies in your family, do not come to ask the church in which you do not believe to come bury him. Go to the sea-side for consolation.[11]

It's not hard in most places to get people interested in Jesus. It's not terribly difficult to get people to make some sort of decision for Jesus. What is hard—here and everywhere—is getting people to stick with Jesus. There will always be a great market for religious experience in our world. There will always be enthusiasm for ambiguously defined spirituality. But what about following Jesus day after day, week after week, year after year? God wants our commitment to be single-minded.

He also wants our commitment to be serious. That was the point Joshua made in the rest of his message to the Israelites (24:23–27). He said, in effect, "If you want to make a real commitment, then throw away the foreign gods. I don't want to just *hear* your commitment. I want to *see* it."

You can almost picture the scene as Joshua spoke. "Who will follow the Lord alone?" *We will, Joshua!* "Are you sure?" *Absolutely.* "Really?" *No doubt about it.* "Well then, throw away those idols." *Gulp.* I wonder if some of them started sweeping the statues behind their backs. *What idols, Joshua?*

Joshua drew up a covenant for them, an agreement, a contract. He didn't settle for the lowest common denominator of religious commitment, a perfunctory tip of the hat toward Yahweh. He made the seriousness of their commitment crystal clear: "This is what I mean. This is what I am saying. Are you sure you want in?"

Seriousness does not mean we are dull and frowny-faced all the time. I've often prayed that I would take myself less seriously, even as I take God more seriously. Serious here isn't the opposite of joyful. It's the opposite of casual. We need to be intentional in our devotion to God, purposeful in our obedience to him. We are high-commitment people in other areas of life, but for some reason not with our faith. We can be workaholics, but then we say Christianity is too much work. We can pursue rigorous recreation, but then we say following Jesus is too hard. We can be on diets and exercise regimens, but then complain that Christian maturity demands too much. Young people plan for education, for marriage, for getting the perfect job, but then figure they don't need to be concerned about their faith until someday when they're older.

I pointed out earlier, in Joshua 23 the Lord had given Israel rest. And that was true. The fighting was done. There was peace. There was some normalcy to their lives. We might say the Israelites had settled down to pay their bills, go grocery shopping, and see their kids play soccer. A nice quiet life. Except that the command that started the book—be strong and courageous (1:6, 9)—reappears here at the end of the book. "Therefore, be very strong to keep and to do all that is written in the Book of the Law of Moses, turning aside from it neither to the right hand nor to the left" (23:6). Apparently, the most difficult task before the Israelites was not crushing their enemies, but subduing the sin in their own hearts.

The choice that matters most is actually a lifetime of choices. The Israelites needed to reaffirm their commitment, even after they were at rest. Perhaps *especially* when they were at rest. The choice they had to make is the same basic choice you still need to make—not just once, but as a way of life. Will you trust in Christ? Will you obey Christ? Will you follow Christ? Will you *keep* following Christ? There is no halfway house here. God wants us all in or all out. Choose this day whom you will serve.

3

The First Day of the Next Chapter of Your Life

I KNOW THAT MANY different ages may be reading this book. I trust you will all be able to glean something from this chapter, but in the next several pages I want to talk specifically to high school graduating seniors. Some of you have heard hundreds of sermons over the years—many of them at church, and for some of you, one sermon a week for the past dozen years in your Christian school. But since you are already reading these pages, you might as well pay attention.[12]

This is a season of milestones for many of you. Final papers and final exams. Last games, last meets, and last classes. You've worked hard to get to this point. And you are probably working hard for what is coming next. For many of you that's college or university. You'll get ready over the summer. You'll buy some dorm furniture. You'll say goodbye to your friends. You'll say goodbye to your parents. You'll find your way around a new school and a new place. You are making preparations for all that lies ahead. After filling out forms, sending in applications, and narrowing down your choices, you finally made your decision. And in a few months, most of you will be somewhere new.

You are probably tired of making decisions. But I want to remind you of one colossal decision that is coming your way. The decision doesn't seem earth shattering. In fact, it seems much less important than the hundred other decisions you've had to make in the last year. This decision is so much an afterthought for most graduating seniors that maybe you've not even considered it yet.

Fast forward a few months from now. You are living on your own—in a dorm or in an apartment somewhere. You've unloaded your stuff. You've met your roommate. You've signed up for classes. You've had a few meals in the cafeteria. You've endured days of awkward orientation activities. And after a short night of sleep on your first Saturday in this new phase of your life, you wake up Sunday morning. What are you going to do?

This is what I want to talk to you about, so please listen carefully: *Of all the decisions you'll face this year, the most im-*

portant one may be whether you get up and go to church on the very first Sunday when no one is there to make sure that you go.

I pastored a church in Michigan that was for many years right across the street from Michigan State University. We saw scores of freshmen visit our church their first Sunday on campus. True, many of them never came back. We saw students who started at church and didn't last. But we rarely saw students who didn't start at church and eventually make it there. What you do in those first weeks on your own, especially what you do with your commitment to a local church, will set you on a trajectory where Jesus Christ will truly be Lord of your life or where he will be something that you learned as a young person and then left behind.

Listen to Jesus

I know, I know. This is what you would expect a pastor to say to you: "Be sure to go to church, young man! Don't sleep in on Sunday, young woman!" You may think, "I'm not against going to church, but isn't my relationship with Jesus the really important thing? I'll still read my Bible even if I don't make it to church." You may be going to a Christian college, and you'll have chapel services and Christian roommates and chaplains wanting to meet with you. Or you will be at schools with Cru or RUF or Campus Outreach.

That's great. Praise God for good campus ministries. Praise God for Christian colleges.

But your chapel is not a church. Your weekly Cru meeting is not a church. Your dorm Bible study is not a church. Remember what Jesus said to Peter in Matthew 16, "You are Peter, and on this rock I will build my church, and the gates of hell shall not prevail against it" (v. 18). Jesus never promised to build up a Christian college. He never promised to build a Christian day school. He never promised to build a campus ministry. There is only one institution on earth that Jesus Christ promised to build, and that's the church.

If you want to be into what Jesus is into, you'll get into a church.

You need to decide before you leave home what you will do on that first Sunday morning. Don't wait until that moment to decide, because you'll probably decide you're tired, or you don't have a car, or you don't know where to go, or you'll get to it next week. Decide before that first Sunday what you will do on that first Sunday. You'll be making all sorts of plans this summer, and one of the most important decisions you may ever make is what you will be committed to that first week and those first months. Will you get up and go to church—not just chapel, not just campus ministry—but a local church, where the people aren't all your age, where the music isn't all your style, where the pastor may not be everything you want him to be?

A Grotesque Anomaly

The British pastor John Stott was not known for overstatement. He was, like a refined English parson, very careful and measured. Which is why these words, written a few years before his death, are so striking. "An unchurched Christian is a grotesque anomaly. The New Testament knows nothing of such a person. For the church lies at the very center of the eternal purpose of God. It is not a divine afterthought."[13]

Think of three of the main images for the church in the New Testament: the church pictured as a building, as a bride, and as a body. Christ is the foundation, and the church is the building. Christ is the groom, and the church is the bride. Christ is the head, and the church is the body. Each pair goes together. You are not meant to have one without the other. We are not meant to have Christ without the church.

Would you want your building to have a foundation but no house?

Would you call it a marriage if there was a groom but no bride?

Would you want to carry around a head without the body?

In Greek mythology, Perseus was the son of Zeus who killed Medusa, the monster-like Gorgon with a head of hair consisting of snakes. You probably remember the story. If anyone looked on Medusa, that person would turn to stone. So, when Perseus went to kill Medusa, he used his shield to look at her reflection so he could approach Medusa in her sleep and cut off her head. Of course, Perseus still couldn't look at her head even though she was dead, so he kept it in a bag, wrapped up so he wouldn't accidentally see it. Later in the story, Perseus defeated the Kraken (a sea monster) by taking Medusa's head out of the bag and holding it out for the sea monster to gaze upon and turn to stone. It's a famous scene depicted in ancient sculptures, in art works, and now in a number of movies.

But it's all rather grotesque when you think about it— carrying around a severed head, lifting up a head without its body. Decapitation is not pretty. If you were into severed heads without their bodies, we would think something was really wrong with you.

Except, it seems, when it comes to our Christian lives. Then we think decapitation is cool.

Some of us even think it is positively good and beautifully spiritual. Too many Christians think they can have Jesus without the church. They want the head without the body. They want a decorpulated Christianity. They want a decapitated Jesus.

A Worldview and a Rhythm of Life

I am willing to bet that at some point growing up you've heard the word "worldview." That word is in the mission statement of almost every Christian school. Teachers and parents want to give students a biblical lens for looking at everything. They want you to be renewed in your minds so that you view the world not just as someone with a great education does but as someone with a distinctly Christian education.

That's all very important. I hope to impart a Christian worldview to my own children. But do you know what may be even more important than getting them to think the right things? It's getting them to instinctively embrace the right rhythms. The most powerful influences in your life are often the things you don't even think about, the things you do out of habit, the things you do because you always do them—whether someone makes you do them or not.

We are formed not just by thoughts but by habits too, study habits, exercise habits, social media habits, personal hygiene habits. These may not be planks in our worldview, but they shape us just as much or even more. It's just what we do. And in time what we do becomes who we are. Will the local church be one of your habits in the next year? There are plenty of lukewarm Christians sitting in churches every week across this country. That's not the goal. But you want to know where you can find passionate, on fire, totally sold-out Christians? In church. In fact, you won't find them anywhere else.

I said at the beginning that this chapter was for high-school seniors in particular, but there are things we all need to hear. No matter who we are, whatever our stage of life, when it comes time to make a decision about where to live or where to go to school or what house to buy, you should put church at the top of your list. And if you're just starting your college search, don't forget to put "church" on your list. What eternal good will it do you if you find a school with a great cafeteria, a great campus, a great sports program, and a great academic pedigree but no great church nearby?

If you're a younger student, you may already be very committed to church. Maybe you go with your parents every week. There is almost no greater blessing they can give you, almost no better privilege, than the habit of attending church faithfully. Try to listen as best you can. Try to go in with a good attitude, even when you're tired or bored. Maybe even ask your parents, "Why aren't we going to church this Sunday?" if they aren't going.

And parents, think about the priorities you are passing down to your children. The good news is you have the biggest influence on whether your child will go to church or not. The bad news is you have the biggest influence on whether your child will go to church or not. Your kids will pick up your walk more than your talk. They will follow the example of a lifetime more than the exhortation you give them when you drop them off at college. Are your kids growing up with the habit of regular church attendance?

It's one of the best things my parents ever did for me: they took me to church every week, Sunday morning and Sunday evening. It wasn't even a question. It wasn't up for debate. It didn't depend upon the weather. It didn't depend on whether we had a full day of activities on Saturday. It didn't depend on whether the sports league had a tournament on Sunday. We went to church, and so it never even crossed my mind that Christians don't go to church. It didn't cross my mind that I would go off to college and not go to church. It's what we did. It's who we were. It was a non-negotiable rhythm of life. And today, I'm hugely grateful for this.

Let me conclude with this prediction, which I think is not only supported by personal experience but also by the word of God: if you want to be much less of a follower of Jesus Christ five years from now, make church marginal in your life. If you make church an afterthought, you won't be thinking about centering your life on Jesus five years from now.

Therefore, don't give up meeting together as some are in the habit of doing (Heb. 10:25). Ephesians 1 says, God "put all things under his feet and gave him as head over all things to the church, which is his body, the fullness of him who fills all in all" (vv. 22–23). Don't cut the head off of Jesus. Decide today that you will get up on that first Sunday morning and find a good gospel-preaching, Bible-believing church. To be sure, we can meet with God anywhere. But only in the church do we have the *fullness* of him who fills all in all.

4

Two Ways to Live

I WANT TO TELL YOU A STORY—a true story. It's about a young man who, at the age of eighteen, went off to school. His family background was difficult. His mother was a Christian and his father, who had died when he was sixteen, had not been. When this young man went off to school, he did what many students do. He threw off the faith he had grown up with, laughing at the teachings of the church. He wandered down all sorts of religious dead ends.

This young student was a good communicator and extremely smart, but he had two crippling vices. First, he was terribly proud. He studied hard to be the best so others could see he was the best. His passion was not learning for the sake of knowledge but learning to impress people and amaze them with his intellect. He was a man quite full of himself and far too smart, he thought, for Christianity. Reflecting upon this time of life years later, he recognized that he was puffed with pride. He was only a beginner, but he fancied himself a sophisticated thinker and a mature adult.

His second vice was a lust for sex and sexuality. Like many teenagers, his mind was sound, but his hormones made him stupid. He was so in love with erotic love that his soul was rotting from the inside out. He said, "To me it was sweet to love and be loved, the more so if I could also enjoy the body of the beloved."[14] The single desire that dominated his young life was simply to love and to be loved. Unfortunately, his passions clouded his heart so that he could not see "the difference between love's serenity and lust's darkness."[15]

For the next several years, this young man traveled farther and farther away from God and more and more into "unhappiness, proud in my self-pity, incapable of rest in my exhaustion."[16] His life was a mess. He was looking for love in all the wrong places. He was filling up his soul with salt water. He was carrying his hopes and dreams in leaky buckets. And it wasn't until he was in his thirties that God sovereignly and miraculously drew him back to himself.

You may have heard of this man before. His name is Augustine (354–430), the bishop of Hippo in North Africa who became the most influential theologian in the history of the church. God made a saint and a scholar out of a sex-crazed teenager.

By God's grace, Augustine ended up on the right path. But it took him a while to get there, and the path he was on (many paths actually) was leading him away from joy, away from satisfaction, away from the good, the true, and the beautiful. The life of Augustine reminds us that there are two ways to live. There is a way that looks like blessing but in the end leads to death, and a way that is more difficult at first but in the end leads to life.

The Way of Blessing

Many texts in the Bible highlight the difference between these two ways to live. One of the clearest is Psalm 1.

> Blessed is the man
> who walks not in the counsel of the wicked,
> nor stands in the way of sinners,
> nor sits in the seat of scoffers;
> but his delight is in the law of the LORD,
> and on his law he meditates day and night.

> He is like a tree
> planted by streams of water

that yields its fruit in its season,
    and its leaf does not wither.
In all that he does, he prospers.
The wicked are not so,
    but are like chaff that the wind drives away.

Therefore the wicked will not stand in the judgment,
    nor sinners in the congregation of the righteous;
for the Lord knows the way of the righteous,
    but the way of the wicked will perish.

It's fitting that Psalm 1 begins, and the whole Psalter begins, with a blessing. The Hebrew word is *asher*, and "blessed" is a good translation of the word. But "blessed" can sound so spiritual that we miss the point of the passage. The word *asher* also means happy or happiness. It's the word the Queen of Sheba used when she visited Solomon in 1 Kings 10:8: "How happy your people must be! How happy your officials, who continually stand before you and hear your wisdom!" (NIV). When you hear "blessed" at the beginning of Psalm 1, don't think in terms of rewards (i.e., if you live like this, you will get this blessing in return). Think: "How happy are those who live like this!" "How good it is to be the man described in this Psalm!" "This is the way to live!"

Psalm 1 shows us the blessed and happy way to live by outlining three negatives, one positive, two metaphors, and a conclusion.

Three Negatives (Ps. 1:1)

To understand verse 1, we need to know something about Hebrew poetry. Hebrew poetry is full of parallelism. That means instead of saying "the trees are tall," Hebrew poetry says, "The trees are tall; the cedars stretch to the heavens." They state the same idea twice, but in slightly different ways. This parallelism is used thousands of times in the Psalms. For example:

- "Lord, how many are my foes! How many rise up against me!" (Ps. 3:1 NIV).
- "Give ear to my words, O Lord, consider my groaning" (Ps. 5:1).
- "Lord, rebuke me not in your anger, nor discipline me in your wrath" (Ps. 6:1).

This is the kind of parallelism we have in Psalm1:1. The three negatives in verse 1 are three ways of saying the same thing: don't be wicked.

And yet, the parallel statements aren't mere repetition. Each line adds a twist. The three verbs show progression. First the man is walking, then standing, then sitting. The progression is from casual acquaintance with sin, to participation in sin, to entrapment by sin. That's how sin works. The blessed man realizes that little sins lead to bigger sins. The wise man knows that if you play with fire you are going to get burned (Prov. 6:27–28). Sin does not want part of us. Sin wants *all* of us. The devil lies to us and tells us that a little sin will make us more of a person, more of a manly man, more of an attractive woman. But the truth is that sin wants mastery over you. Sin wants to turn your walking into standing and your standing into sitting.

There's another progression of sin in verse 1. When you are living the wrong way, first you take counsel from the wicked, then you begin to act like the wicked, and finally you join the wicked. The progression is from thinking to behaving to belonging. What starts out as a bad idea from a bad person ends up shaping who you hang out with and who you are. Obviously, this doesn't mean you never talk to a non-Christian or befriend an immoral person. But we must be on our guard; bad company corrupts good character (1 Cor. 15:33). A little leaven works through the whole batch of dough (Gal. 5:9). If you think like a fool, you will soon act like a fool, and eventually you will join the fools.

Be very careful that you do not end up where verse 1 ends up; namely, sitting in the seat of scoffers. Our culture loves mockers. We are entertained by cynical people. Their dry pessimism can draw a crowd. They make us laugh. Mockers are cool. They are so cool, they don't believe anything. Nothing gets to them. They are so hip they can look down on the world of simpletons. Everything is a joke, and religious people are rubes. That's the heart of the scoffer. And if you ever find yourself in that place, you should cry out to God for mercy because your heart has gotten very hard. There are lots of smart people who are religious fools. They may have plenty of degrees and know how to use fancy words, but they are not wise. And they are not blessed. Walking in wickedness and mockery is no way to live.

One Positive (Ps. 1:2)

Sometimes people say, "I don't want a religion with its institutions, and doctrines, and rules. I just want a relationship with Jesus." That sounds pious, but it is false. The Psalmist says precisely the opposite. "Blessed is the man who delights in the law of the Lord." That's the one positive quality mentioned of the blessed man. The happy man says "O give me that book. Let me read it. Let me study it. Let me pray through it and meditate on it. My soul thrills to pore over God's word because it reveals God. Oh, how I love the law of the Lord!"

Have you ever thought about how strange this sounds—delighting in the law of the Lord? We can understand delighting in the love of the Lord, or the light of the Lord, but the law of the Lord? C. S. Lewis confessed that delighting in the law was at first mysterious to him:

> I can understand that a man can, and must, respect these "statutes," and try to obey them, and assent to them in his heart. But it is very hard to find how they could be, so to speak, delicious, how they exhilarate . . . surely it (a statute) could be more aptly compared to the dentist's forceps or the front line than to anything enjoyable and sweet.[17]

Lewis articulates how many people naturally feel about the commandments of God. But the blessed man is cheered and gladdened and pleased to hear God's law.

God's word is more to be desired than gold, than much fine gold; and sweeter than honey from the honeycomb (Ps. 19:10). And why is this so? Lewis argues that, among other blessings, "delight in the Law is a delight in having touched firmness; like the pedestrian's delight in feeling the hard road beneath his feet after a false shortcut has long entangled him in muddy fields."[18] Lewis is right: if you've ever tried taking a shortcut and found yourself traipsing through the muck and the mire, you know how glad you are to emerge from the squishy bog and hit pavement again. You feel like you can run again, like you can move, like you're free because you have touched firmness again.

That's the law of the Lord. It's something hard and solid in a world where everything is unsure and uncertain. It's a sure path. He who truly loves God will love God's word because the word reveals God and sets us on firm ground. That's the best way to live. That's God's way to live. "For the mind that is set on the flesh is hostile to God, for it does not submit to God's law; indeed, it cannot" (Rom. 8:7). But the mind that is quickened by the Spirit delights in the law of the Lord and meditates on it day and night.

Two Metaphors (Ps. 1:3–4)

These two ways to live can be pictured in two metaphors. The first metaphor has to do with trees and involves two related aspects of tree-dom. The happy man is like a tree because (1) he has the endurance of a tree, and (2) he has the fruitfulness of a tree.

Let's start with the endurance. If you live God's way, you will not be blown over when the storms come. Notice, I did not say *if* the storms come. I did not say you will be spared from the storms. The promise here is not that the righteous will have a life free of difficulties. Read the rest of the Psalms, and you'll know that's not true. The promise is that if you live God's way, you'll be rooted. Endurance is not a magic spell that falls upon the Christian. Endurance comes from knowing what God's word requires, knowing who we are according to God's word, and knowing that God's word lasts when all else falters and fails.

The blessed man who delights in the law of the Lord also has the fruitfulness of a tree. And notice the phrase: "that yields its fruit *in its season.*" There is a quiet growth in the godly man or woman. You don't have to be fancy or successful. If you have healthy roots, in time, the Lord will make you blossom. The Lord will give you fruit. He will give you life. And in season, people will see it.

You and I need to make decisions for the long term, not the short term. You've probably seen those motivational posters before—the kind of cheesy posters hanging in some office cubicle with the word "Teamwork" or "Integrity" or "Leadership" and an inspiring picture of people climbing mountains together. Whether anyone in the history of the planet has actually been inspired by those posters, I'll let you decide. The posters are so cliché, they have spawned a whole series of de-motivational posters, which if not more inspiring are at least funnier. One of the best ones has a picture of a man standing at the edge of a cliff overlooking some clouds with the caption that says, "Procrastination. Hard work often pays off after time, but laziness always pays off now." I suppose many college students have set out to prove that the poster is true!

But even if you are in the habit of cramming for tests and turning in papers at the last minute, please don't be the sort of person who only makes decisions with the short term in view. We think we have so much figured out when we are twenty years old, but we don't know what we don't know. And one of the things we tend not to know is how to think not just in terms of weeks and months but also of years and decades. The wise and happy person (in the long run) is the person who learns to practice delayed gratification, the person who chooses what is harder now for what is better later. In a world that encourages us to be short-lived flowers and flimsy grass, let's make a commitment to be sturdy trees.

That's the first metaphor. The blessed person is a like a tree that lasts and a tree that bears fruit. The second metaphor also comes from the world of agriculture. If the wise person is like a tree, the foolish person is like chaff.

Chaff is the non-seed part of grain. It's what gets thrown out. It's light and insignificant and blown away by the wind. In the ancient world, they would often separate the wheat from the chaff by throwing the threshed grain into the air. The heavier, good part of the grain would fall to the ground to be kept, while the light stuff—husks and debris—would be blown away by the wind. Chaff was both worthless and weightless.

Our world specializes in light and trivial. Everywhere people are famous for being famous. People look impressive. They seem important. They think they're important. But they ignore the eternity in their hearts (Eccles. 3:11). They give no thought to their souls. They seem consequential, but measured by the things that really matter, they're living hollow, weightless, insignificant lives.

Don't be fooled. People are people. Professors, jocks, beauty queens, the rich, the poor, the politicians—they all come from the dust and will return to the dust. We are not as strong as we think we are. And the Lord is not as weak as we imagine him to be. Plant your roots by the streams of living water, and you can be stronger than you know. Walk in the ways of the wicked, and you will forever be less than you could have been.

Conclusion (Ps. 1:5–6)

In the Psalmist's conclusion he looks past this earthly life into eternal life. The wicked who stand now in the way of sinners, will not stand in the judgment to come. The sinners who sit in the seat of mockers now, will not sit in the assembly of the righteous later. There are two ways to live. The way of the sinners will perish, but the Lord will watch over the way of the righteous.

Notice what verse 6 says. The Lord *knows* the way of the righteous. If we paid attention to that word, it would be such a help to us. When your brother gets diagnosed with throat cancer, the Lord knows. When your family is far away, and it makes you want to cry, the Lord knows. When your whole week gives you one sleepless night after another, the Lord knows.

Crucially, as Christians we know that the Lord's knowledge is not a mere head knowledge about our circumstances. On the other side of the incarnation, we can see that the Lord not only knows the blessed man of Psalm 1, he is the blessed man. The Lord knows the way of the righteous because he has walked the righteous way. More than that, he is the way. As Jesus said in John 14:6, "I am the way, the truth, and the life, and no one comes to the Father except through me." The way of blessing is the way of Jesus. Live your life in Jesus, for Jesus, following Jesus. That's the best, blessed, most delightful way to live.

After all his wanderings, Augustine found the way to be truly happy:

There is a delight which is given not to the wicked, but to those who worship you for no reward save the joy that you yourself are to them. That is the authentic happy life, to set one's joy on you, grounded in you and caused by you. That is the real thing, and there is no other. Those who think that the happy life is found elsewhere, pursue another joy and not the true one.[19]

Augustine eventually came around to walk in the way of blessing. Will you?

Horseshoes, Hand Grenades, and the Kingdom of God

"CLOSE ONLY COUNTS in horseshoes and hand grenades."

For some reason, I grew up hearing that aphorism. I say "for some reason" because I've never been much acquainted with horseshoes, and I've been even less familiar with hand grenades. But foreign as both objects might be to you, the saying isn't hard to understand. Close may be good enough when playing the game of horseshoes and when trying to blow stuff up, but in other areas of life, close doesn't count for anything.

This is certainly true when it comes to the kingdom of God. In fact, there's a story about this in the Gospels. Close might make you a winner at throwing horseshoes, and it might make you a dangerous soldier wielding a hand grenade, but when it comes to the kingdom, close isn't good enough for Jesus. Close is better than far, but it's still just close. And—if you'll forgive the poor grammar—close ain't in.

Here's how the Gospel of Mark makes this point.

And one of the scribes came up and heard them disputing with one another, and seeing that he answered them well, asked him, "Which commandment is the most important of all?" Jesus answered, "The most important is 'Hear, O Israel: The Lord our God, the Lord is one. And you shall love the Lord your God will all your heart and with all your soul and with all your mind and with all your strength.' The second is this: 'You shall love your neighbor as yourself.' There is no other commandment greater than these." And the scribe said to him, "You are right, Teacher. You have truly said that he is one, and there is no other besides him. And to love him with all the heart and with all the understanding and with all the strength, and to love one's neighbor as oneself, is much more than all whole burnt offerings and sacrifices." And when Jesus saw that he answered wisely, he said to him, "You are not far from the kingdom of God." And after that no one dared to ask him any more questions. (Mark 12:28–34)

Good news for the scribe: he's close. Bad news for the scribe: he's not in. That may be the same good news/bad news for you. So let's try to understand what's going on in this passage.

A Familiar Debate

The scribe came to Jesus with a question: "Which commandment is most important of all?" This was not an unusual question. According to tradition, there are 613 commandments in the Torah, so it was natural that people would try to find some unifying principle or establish some system for ranking the commandments. The Rabbis thought all the commandments needed to be obeyed, but there were lighter matters and weightier matters of the law. Jesus used this same language at times. This whole business of finding the most important commandment was not idle curiosity. It was a significant question for the Jews, and Jesus treated it as such.

From other historical documents, we know that the Rabbis had dealt with this question before. A generation before Jesus was on the scene, there's a famous story about a popular Rabbi named Hillel. Someone once asked him, "Teach me the whole Torah while I am standing on one leg." In other words, "Give me your best, most succinct summary of the law. I only have a minute here, so tell me what I really need to know." The scribe in Mark's Gospel was asking Jesus a similar question. Asking about the most important commandment was not an uncommon question.

And Jesus gave a pretty traditional response. We sometimes think of Jesus as being in constant friction with Judaism. But he wasn't. Up until the end, he was popular with the masses (even if they didn't fully understand who he was). Many of the leaders despised him, but not all. And while Jesus certainly saw himself fulfilling the law and, in some ways, transcending it, he fully embraced being a Jew and fully believed in obeying the Hebrew Scriptures (what we call the Old Testament).

Jesus answered the scribe by quoting from Deuteronomy 6:4–5. This passage was the John 3:16 for the Jews and their Bible. When we think of the famous parts of the Old Testament, we might think of Psalm 23 or the Daniel and the lions' den story, but nothing was more important for the Jews than Deuteronomy 6:4–5. It's called "the Shema" because *shema* is the Hebrew word for "hear" (as in "Hear, O Israel"). A good Jew recited the Shema every day, and probably heard it in the temple and in the synagogue every week. Everyone knew the Shema. If they had them in the ancient world, the Jews would have held up the Shema at soccer games and put it on birthday cakes.

In other words, Jesus was giving a standard, acceptable answer to the scribe's question. "The most important command is to love God with everything you've got. Love him with your decisions. Love him with your affections. Love him with your thinking. Love him with your actions. There is only one God, and you ought to love him from the top of your head to the tip of your toes. That's the greatest commandment."

Then Jesus mentioned one more command. He quoted from Leviticus 19:18. This too was a well-known verse. When the people asked Hillel to summarize the Torah, he gave a variation on the Golden Rule: "Do not do to your neighbor what is hateful to you; this is the whole Torah: the rest is commentary."[20] The first-century Jewish philosopher Philo also talked about our double duty to love God and love our neighbor. While no one may have put Deuteronomy 6 and Leviticus 19 together exactly as Jesus did, the two ideas were common enough.

The Jews looked at the Ten Commandments as having two parts: the first part dealt with our relationship to God and the second part with our relationship to each other. These are the so-called two tables of the law. Deuteronomy 6 and Leviticus 19 are appropriate summaries of these two tables: "Love God first, and then love your neighbor too. That's the whole point of the law." Jesus wasn't suggesting you could throw out the rest of the 611 commandments. You needed the whole law to tell you what love for God and love for neighbor looked like. But as a condensed version of the law, as a matter of first things, these were the most important commandments.

Love the Lord your God; love your neighbor as yourself. That's what Jesus taught, and that's what many of the Jews would have believed. In fact, many people all around the world, from various religions, would still agree that this is a good summary of what God desires from his people.

Impressed and Impressive

The scribe was impressed with Jesus's answer. This was surprising. Not because of the answer itself, but because no member of the religious elite had dared to side with Jesus during the temple conflicts. After the triumphal entry at the beginning of chapter 11, Mark outlines a series of debates with Jesus in and around the temple. There was controversy about the temple, about the authority of Jesus, about taxes to Caesar, about the resurrection, and now about the law. In every instance, except this last one, the religious leaders stood opposed to Jesus, and Jesus provoked the religious leaders. At the end of chapter 12, Jesus warned everyone to "beware of the scribes" (v. 38), so it's surprising that Jesus and the scribe got along as well as they did in their conversation about the commandments.

The surprise is amplified when we consider that the scribes, as a class of people in the Gospels, are normally defenders of the status quo. They are akin to academics and lawyers in our day. The scribes were experts in the law and loyal to the temple. It's remarkable, then, that this scribe recognized that love is more important than religious ritual. He likely knew Hosea 6:6—"I desire steadfast love and not sacrifice, the knowledge of God rather than burnt offerings." The priority of love was an Old Testament idea, but for a scribe to admit this, especially in the hostile setting leading up to Jesus's death, is noteworthy. This was a surprisingly friendly, surprisingly wise scribe.

The scribe was impressed with Jesus, and Jesus was impressed with the scribe (v. 34). The scribe was right to believe that Jesus was right. Jesus said to him, in effect, "You are well on your way to being the sort of person that is accepted in God's kingdom." Of course, Jesus was not talking about a geographical or political kingdom. He was talking about a spiritual kingdom. Jesus was saying, "You are not far from joining God's team. You're not far from inheriting eternal life."

First the Good News

What Jesus told the scribe was meant as a compliment. And deservedly so. Think of everything the scribe got right.

First, he believed that God exists and there is only one God. More than that, as a Jewish scribe, we can be sure he didn't believe in a generic, deistic God. This man believed that the God of Israel created the world. He believed in a God who knew everything, could do anything, and ruled over everything. The God of Israel was one, and this one God was the only God.

Second, the scribe knew the importance of loving God. The Lord was not just to be feared or worshiped but also to be loved. This man wanted to love God with everything he had. What's more, he understood that love could not be reduced to an emotional feeling. Loving God involves your desires, your intellect, your attitude, your behavior. As the first and greatest priority in his life, the scribe believed in loving the Lord his God.

Third, the scribe knew the importance of loving his neighbors. We might say this man wanted to be a good person. He wanted to help others. He knew that love required sacrifices. He was committed to loving his neighbor as much as he was concerned for himself.

Fourth, the scribe understood the importance of the heart. "If I bring the right animals to the temple," he acknowledged, "and I get all the rituals right, but I don't really love God in my heart, then what does it matter?" This man knew that it was possible to look religious without actually being close to God.

Fifth, the scribe has a favorable impression of Jesus. Mark 12:28 tells us that the scribe approached Jesus in the first place because he saw that Jesus had answered everyone's questions very well. As an expert in the Bible, the scribe knew a good teacher when he heard one. He could see that Jesus knew his stuff. We might even say the scribe was a fan of Jesus. Given all the opposition to Jesus in these chapters, it took a lot of courage and humility for the scribe to approach Jesus and commend Jesus as a friend instead of as a foe.

For all this, Jesus gave the man a remarkable commendation. Jesus hasn't had anything good to say to anyone all day. Jesus never talked to scribes like this elsewhere in the Gospel of Mark. But Jesus liked this man. This man was really close to getting it.

And that may be where you are at. You may be getting closer to Jesus. You may be inching toward the kingdom. You've decided there is a God, and you genuinely want to have a relationship with him. You realize you can't keep living the way you are living. You want to help people. You have a desire to make a difference for good in the world. You are tired of going through the motions. You have a deep respect for Jesus. If that describes you, you are on the right track. The good news is: you're close.

Then the Bad News

But here's the bad news: close ain't in. For all the scribe's impressive credentials and for all his impressive statements, he was not yet in the kingdom. This man seemed to have it all put together. And yet, Jesus said, in his present position, the scribe will not inherit the kingdom of God. This is a warning you may need to hear. There are a lot of church-going people who think they are in, but they're only *close* to being in.

Let's look at this scribe one more time and notice again all that he has going for him.

- He had a basic theistic worldview. He believed in a personal, Creator God. The man was a monotheist. He recognized the simplicity and singularity of Israel's God.
- He believed Scripture. He affirmed the authority of Deuteronomy and Leviticus as much as Jesus did. He had committed his life to studying Scripture.
- He exemplified basic moral principles. He was a decent man—honest, humble, searching, likeable.

- He understood true religion is more than mere formalism. He was sincere. He had an inner piety. He wanted to be "spiritual" not just "religious."
- He had probably been surrounded by God's people his whole life. He had been part of the covenant community. He had been deep in the worship of the true God. As a first-century Jew, he likely grew up in a seriously religious family.
- He had nothing but good things to say about Jesus. Even when his peers argued with Jesus, he believed Jesus was a good man and a wise teacher. The scribe was boldly pro-Jesus.

Perhaps this description of the scribe is also a description of you: you believe in God, you believe in the Bible, you believe in morality, you believe that true religion is a matter of the heart, you have been surrounded by the truth your whole life, you are a sincere and spiritual person, you even have a very positive view of Jesus. If this describes you, that's good; that's better than a lot of other things that could describe a person.

But remember, the scribe was only close to the kingdom of God.

Perhaps you have been at the doorstep of the kingdom your whole life. You've convinced yourself that you are in.

People may have even treated you like you were in. But now as you enter this new phase of life, you need to ask yourself: "Am I close, or am I in?" The scribe was close, but close only counts in horseshoes and hand grenades.

The Missing Link

So what was missing? If the scribe was not far from the kingdom, what was necessary to bring him all the way there? The answer is what Jesus taught next. In Mark 12:35–37 Jesus intentionally referenced the scribes. "How can the scribes say that the Christ is the son of David?" Jesus asked. He then quoted from Psalm 110, making the point that David calls the Christ his Lord. So which is it—is the Messiah David's Son or David's Lord? Of course, the answer is both. The Christ was not only a descendant of King David, he is David's divine King.

Once we realize that Jesus will soon—finally and fully—acknowledge that he is the Christ (14:61–62), we can see what he is up to. Jesus is David's son and David's Lord. Jesus is the one about whom the prophets spoke. Jesus is the one with all authority in heaven and on earth. To affirm the Shema was one thing, but Jesus was putting himself in the middle of the Shema as the object of love and worship (cf. 1 Cor. 8:4–6). The difference between being close and being in is bowing the knee to Jesus. The one entry point into the kingdom is to believe in the marvelous stone that the builders have rejected (Mark 12:10–11).

This may sound easy enough: just believe in Jesus. But remember "believing" in Jesus is not the same as liking Jesus or being a fan of Jesus. The scribe already liked Jesus. Lots of people in the Gospels liked Jesus. They followed him from place to place, marveled at his works, and were astonished by his teaching. They were into Jesus. But they were not fully committed to him. They were not ready to lay down their lives to follow him. They were not willing to embrace the scandal and the shame of being associated with one who would die on a cross. Many people today are happy to be vaguely supportive of Jesus, but they don't want to go all the way and obey everything he taught, believe everything he said, become a member of his church, and count everything as loss for the sake of Christ.

Believing in Jesus—truly believing in Jesus—is also difficult because it means death to justification by law keeping. The rich young man in Mark 10 is not a story about being willing to give up everything for Jesus. It's a story about the failure of law keeping as a way to eternal life. Keeping the commandments is essential, but it is not the way to get in. You'll never get in just by loving God and loving your neighbor. Jesus is the only person who has ever fully loved God—his heavenly Father—with all his heart, soul, strength, and mind. Jesus is the only one who perfectly loved his neighbor more than he loved himself. You don't live that way, not completely. I certainly don't. Almost all of Jesus's disciples would desert him before his death. That's why he needed to die. God's people have always been rebels and deserters. When it comes to escaping our predicament as sinners, we don't need a strategy; we need a Savior.

The scribe had the right way of looking at the world, and he knew the right things to do, but he had yet to completely trust in the only one who could make him right. Some of you are just getting to know Jesus. Some of you are slowly making your way to Jesus. And some of you have been around Jesus your whole lives. You know him. You even like him. But do you worship him? Is he the functional center in your life? You believe he is Savior and Lord. But perhaps he's not really *your* Savior and Lord. No matter who you are or where you've come from, to all those just sort of hanging around in the vicinity of faith, Jesus says the same thing: "You're close. Why not come in?"

Twelve Old(ish) Books to Read When You Are Young

TALK TO ALMOST any mature, vibrant Christians, and they will tell you about Christian books that have been instrumental in their lives. In fact, one of the best indications I've seen of the Spirit's work in someone's life is that he (or she) develops a newfound love of reading. Granted, many people throughout history have not had the opportunity to learn to read, nor have they had easy access to good books. But thankfully, that is not the predicament you and I are facing. When it comes to good Christian literature, especially written in English or translated into English, we have an embarrassment of riches. There are so many wonderful things to read. The question, for many Christians, then becomes: "Where do I start?"

The answer to that question is virtually endless. But since we have to start somewhere, and since we can't read everything, it can be helpful to get some good recommendations. The list below is not a ranking of the best books in the history of the church. No doubt, the list reflects what influenced me as a young Christian. Thus, it veers heavily toward writers who wrote in English and books that are more oldish than truly old. Nevertheless, the twelve books listed are classics in the best sense of the word—classics not just because they are from another century (I've only listed books written by dead guys), but because they deal with topics that never go out of style and are written in a way that transcends their own time and culture.

One of the most important things we can do when we are young and our beliefs and opinions have not yet fully formed is to make sure we read good books. I hope the annotated bibliography below will help point you in the right direction. I've tried to pick books that are rich and deep, but also accessible and not overly long. For each book I've included the original publication date and a sentence or two of description. I haven't given specific publishing information because most of these works can be easily found in a variety of formats.

1. **Augustine,** *Confessions* (c. 400). There may be no more influential theologian in the history of the

church than Augustine, the bishop of Hippo in North Africa. This autobiographical work traces Augustine's spiritual journey toward Christ through unbelief, philosophical wandering, and sexual promiscuity.

2. **John Calvin, *Golden Booklet of the True Christian Life* (1559).** This little book of devotion and discipleship comes out of Calvin's much larger work *The Institutes of the Christian Religion*. The French theologian and Genevan Reformer provides a beautiful and stirring picture of true spirituality.

3. **Thomas Brooks, *Precious Remedies against Satan's Devices* (1652).** In this work by English preacher and author Thomas Brooks, we see the genius of the Puritans for clearheaded organization, heart-probing spiritual diagnosis, and gospel cure.

4. **John Bunyan, *Pilgrim's Progress* (1678).** This is the most famous Christian allegory ever written and, by some accounts, the most widely distributed book in the world (after the Bible). Bunyan understood the trials and triumphs of the Christian life and presented the journey of faith in a way that has inspired millions of Christians.

5. **J. C. Ryle, *Holiness* (1877).** Ryle, an Anglican bishop in Liverpool, combined a sharp theological mind with unusually crisp communication. This is the best book for understanding the doctrine of progressive sanctification and growing in practical godliness.

6. **G. K. Chesterton, *Orthodoxy* (1908).** From theological treatises to biographies to detective stories, Chesterton was one of the greatest writers in the English language from the twentieth century. This is Chesterton's witty and intellectually robust defense of the joys of Christian orthodoxy.

7. **Herman Bavinck, *The Christian Family* (1908).** Bavinck is best known for his multi-volume *Reformed Dogmatics*, but this exploration of sex, marriage, and family life, though originally written in Dutch over a hundred years ago, remains incredibly relevant for our day.

8. **J. Gresham Machen, *Christianity and Liberalism* (1923).** It's often been said that the most important word in this title is "and." Machen, the Princeton Seminary professor who left to start Westminster

Theological Seminary, argues persuasively that theological liberalism is not a different version of Christianity but a different religion altogether.

9. **C. S. Lewis, *Abolition of Man* (1944).** While Lewis is better known for *Mere Christianity* and *The Chronicles of Narnia*, page for page this is one of the most important things Lewis ever wrote. Lewis argues that in forgetting the God-given natural order of morality, we have made "men without chests" who try to see through first principles and therefore no longer see.

10. **John Murray, *Redemption Accomplished and Applied* (1955).** A Scottish-born pastor and professor, Murray originally wrote this book on the work of Christ and the doctrine of salvation as a series of articles for ordinary church members. You would be hard pressed to find a more succinct and readable theological exploration of the work of Christ and the salvation of sinners.

11. **J. I. Packer, *Knowing God* (1973).** An Anglican clergyman, teacher, and writer, Packer was a master at making theological concepts understandable and explaining them with memorable prose. This

book on the nature and character of God may be the most influential book of serious theology in the past fifty years.

12. **R. C. Sproul, *The Holiness of God* (1985).** No one did more in recent decades to remind us of the bigness of God than R. C. Sproul. This book will make sure we who were created in God's image do not recreate him in ours.

Notes

1. Quindlen made these remarks at Sarah Lawrence College in 2002. They were then published in her book *Loud and Clear* (New York: Random House, 2004), 307.
2. This chapter is adapted from a commencement address I gave: "Whatever You Do, Do Not Be True to Yourself" (Geneva College, Beaver Falls, PA, May 7, 2022), https://kevindeyoung.org.
3. See Carl Trueman, *The Rise and the Triumph of the Modern Self: Cultural Amnesia, Expressive Individualism, and the Road to the Sexual Revolution* (Wheaton, IL: Crossway, 2020).
4. Idina Menzel, "Let It Go" in *Frozen*, directed by Chris Buck and Jennifer Lee (Burbank, CA: Walt Disney Animation Studios, 2013).
5. G. K. Chesterton, *Orthodoxy* (New York: Image, 1959), 75–76.
6. Collin Garbarino, "A Turn for the Worse: *Turning Red* Abandons the Tradition That Made Pixar Great," *WORLD*, March 24, 2022, https://wng.org.
7. *Turning Red*, directed by Domee Shi (Burbank, CA: Walt Disney Pictures; Emeryville, CA: Pixar Animation Studios, 2022).
8. *Brave*, directed by Mark Andrews, Brenda Chapman, and Steve Purcell (Burbank, CA: Walt Disney Pictures; Emeryville, CA: Pixar Animation Studios, 2012).

9. Quindlen, *Loud and Clear*, 307.

10. Rich Mullins, "The Maker of Noses," track 7 on *The World as Best as I Remember It* (vol. 2), 1993.

11. Iain Murray, *D. Martyn Lloyd-Jones: The First Forty Years, 1899–1939* (Edinburgh: Banner of Truth, 1982), 138.

12. This chapter is adapted from my speech to Covenant Day School Matthews, NC, and my following article "The Most Important Decision You're Probably Not Thinking About," TGC (blog), May 24, 2021, https://www.thegospelcoalition.org.

13. John Stott, *Living Church: Convictions of a Lifelong Pastor* (Downers Grove, IL: IVP, 2007), 19.

14. Augustine, *Confessions*, trans. Henry Chadwick (Oxford: Oxford University Press, 1991), 35.

15. Augustine, *Confessions,* 24.

16. Augustine, *Confessions*, 25.

17. C. S. Lewis, *Reflections on the Psalms* (San Diego, CA: Harcourt, 1958), 55.

18. Lewis, *Reflections on the Psalms*, 62.

19. Augustine, *Confessions*, 198–99.

20. Hillel, *Babylonian Talmud*, Shabbat, 31a.

Scripture Index

Scripture Index

Clearly Reformed

Theology for the Everyday

Learn and grow with thousands of resources
from the ministry of Kevin DeYoung.

Browse articles, sermons, books, podcasts,
and more at **clearlyreformed.org**.

Also Available from Kevin DeYoung

For more information, visit **crossway.org**.